# 500 Hours

By

Ronnie Hall

# Author's Dedication


First and foremost, this book is dedicated to

To my Lord and Savior, Jesus Christ

Secondly, this book is dedicated to the men and women of
the Norfolk Police Department

Norfolk Virginia

# Acknowledgment

I am so grateful to my family, who has always stood by me in all my endeavors. To my wife Diane and six of the most wonderful children in the world. Charlene, Kelly, Veronica, Whitney, Ronnie Jr., and my baby girl April.

My mother and father were instrumental in the development of me being the man I am today. I love you, Mom and Dad.

Isaac and Mary Hall

To my lovely 3 sisters

Geneva, Sylvia, and Patricia

To five of the strongest men, I have ever known. My brothers

Cleo, Isaac III, Ralph, Larry, and Gary

To my Heart who raised me the first 18 years of my life

My grandmother

Jennie Owens Scott Bell

I owe you so much! Thanks for loving me

Thank you, Chaplain Terry, for your strong
leadership.

To my brothers who stand with me in the
chaplain's corps, thanks so much for your
brotherhood.

To the International Conference of Police
Chaplains

Thanks for your outstanding police chaplains
training

# Contents

# Preface
# A Police Chaplain's Ride-Along Experience

This book is written following Five-Hundred hours of riding with some of the most professional Police Officers under God's Heaven. These hometown heroes that I am referring to are the men and women of the Norfolk Police Department in Norfolk, Virginia. I pray this book will encourage Police Chaplains, Clergy, City Officials, and Community leaders to spend quality time conducting ride-along with their local law enforcement agencies.

Our country is desperately in need of building stronger relationships between law enforcement and our local communities. Riding

8

with your local police or sheriff's department allows clergy and the community to build strong bridges that will bind the two entities together. I believe in the saying; Together, Everyone Achieves More. Working together first allows the community to become better familiar with the law enforcement officer's world. Secondly, it establishes more trust between law enforcement officers and the community they are sworn to serve.

For the new Chaplains, this book is aimed at helping you navigate a myriad of police customs and courtesies to give you a better understanding of the day-to-day operation of the law enforcement officers' world. Ride Along will help both the new and experienced chaplains build strong bridges to enhance better communication, understanding, and, most of all, trust. Trust will allow the chaplain to do his or her primary job., The focus of the police chaplain is to introduce the spirit of God through a **Ministry of Presence.**

# Introduction

July 9th, 2020, was one of the most exciting days of my life. Six months of waiting had finally ended. My wait was a longing to join the Chaplains Corps of the Norfolk Police Department, Norfolk, Virginia. The senior chaplain had invited me to a Dr. Martin Luther King Jr. March in January of that year to meet the Chief of Police. She wanted to introduce me to the chief and get his approval to bring me on as the newest chaplain for the department.

The senior chaplain felt I would truly be an asset to the Chaplains Corps. After meeting the chief of police, I got excited when the chief approved the senior chaplain to allow me to march alongside her, the chief, the Mayor, the

City Council, and about one hundred members of the community.

I felt blessed, and it was a true honor to be part of the 2020 Norfolk, Virginia, Martin Luther King Jr. birthday march. After the march had concluded, the senior chaplain got the chief's approval to start my application process. The paperwork process did not take long, but the approval period took several months. During the waiting of the application process, the senior chaplain allowed me to shadow her during several police chaplain events. Finally, in July 2020, my application was approved.

The approval notification came with a beautiful welcome aboard card presented by the captain, who was a patrol division commanding officer and the senior leader of the Chaplains

Corps. Her welcome to the police department was spirit-lifting, and I knew from her words of expression she was a believer and a servant of God.

As the newest chaplain, I was filled with both joy and excitement. Nevertheless, my excitement soon turned from joy to sadness as our senior chaplain shared the dreadful news that all chaplain Ride-along had been canceled. Our senior chaplain had worked several months trying to bring our police officers and chaplains together by conducting a ride-along.

Covid-19 had taken a fatal toll on our city, and several of our officers had fallen ill from this horrific Virus. Although we were not happy with the closing of the ride-along, we all understood the seriousness of Covid-19 and the effect it had on our city and our Police Department.

As a police chaplain, my ultimate belief was and still is today that ride-along is the linchpin of police chaplaincy. There is no better way for a chaplain to get to know his or her officers than to ride with them.

As I waited for the Ride-Along ban to be lifted, I focused my efforts on the other areas of police chaplaincy. Police Roll Calls, Promotions, Graduations, Funerals, Police officers' baby births, hospital visits, weddings, phone calls, death notifications, and police department counseling.

At the end of June 2021, God answered my prayer! The ban on ride-along was lifted. As the ban ended, I turned my efforts to prepare for my first ride-along. My adrenaline was on super high, and a million thoughts came rushing through my mind. I knew safety should be the first goal on my things-to-do list.

For my first act, I reported to the Police Departments Property and Evidence Division to be fitted for a Police Protective Vest. After attending so many roll calls and hearing so many discussions concerning protective vests, I knew it was important to have a properly fitted vest. Without a properly fitted Police Protected Vest, no Chaplain ride-along should be conducted. I knew my wait was over, but now I wanted to make sure I was truly prepared for my first ride.

# Chapter 1
# Flashback

Many of You reading this book must have heard about chaplains somewhere around you, in your community, or a professional organization. But that might lead to a question about what chaplains are and why there is a need for them.

Chaplains provide spiritual, emotional, religious, or existential support to people who do not have the privilege to attend regular and organized services of religion due to health, profession, or various other circumstances. Chaplains are usually appointed for a secular setting or location.

The word 'secular' here means places like hospitals, palliative care, sports team, military, workplaces, prisons, schools, colleges, universities, etc. The main role is to listen, care or speak to people of any faith or the ones who do not have faith. Their purpose is to provide help and care to those who need counseling. Chaplains have the desire to support individuals who are struggling in their life.

Like in hospitals, professional therapists, doctors, or nurses, have the responsibility to help heal the medical issues of their patients. This is where chaplains come into the picture. The goal of a chaplain is to spend their time and energy in deep listening when it is needed most. They listen profoundly and empathize with the situation of the person, encouraging them to find real meaning in life.

Chaplains are mainly associated with the church and work in all locations or events outside the church. In all the places they work, their goal is to show God's love by showing care and love offering their support by representing Christian beliefs and values.

Because our society is so diverse, chaplains must express great sensitivity and pure respect for every religion, culture, and school of thought. However, their care, love, and respect always portray the love of God no matter what their faith is. Most likely, chaplains are needed for stressful professions or people dealing with health problems or grievances.

For police service, it has been realized right from the early days that their nature of work is stressful and dehumanizing. In the beginning, the services of the local clergy were utilized to provide support to the staff and maintain a balanced perspective of life.

If you talk about today's police service, it is getting more challenging with time, and now it has been observed that stressful situations are manifesting adverse consequences on the officers. That is why it is recognized that every individual might need some extra help to be able to keep everything in perspective. Every person has their own body, mindset, and spirit, which makes them a complete person. And every human being at times gets affected by dealing with frequent traumatic experiences.

People have this perception about the military and police officers that whatever they do, is part of their job. However, if you work closely with them, you will realize that these men and women can become affected by their nature of work. They see and experience the worst of the worst situations throughout their career. Police officers sometimes must use their weapons which could result in death. When this happens, they must carry this weight throughout their lives. For this purpose, they receive counseling from professionals like doctors and therapists, but they can also receive spiritual counseling from chaplains.

Police officers protect and serve the country, but it is also important for every officer to protect themselves. We all must realize that these officers have families of their very own. Many days at the conclusion of their shift, these officers arrive home with the baggage of guilt, camouflaging their emotions and acting normal to their families. This guilt needs to be freed up so the police officers can do their jobs perfectly, i.e., to serve and protect the community with complete dedication. Chaplains fall into the picture to fulfill the need to liberate officers from all the stress and strains, encouraging them to continue with the fullness of life.

After several conversations with Chaplain Terry, I decided to become a police chaplain. She shared with me the need to be there for our police officers during some of their most challenging times, especially when there is a reporting of a child's injury or death.

These situations take a huge toll on the police officer's mental health.

In one of our conversations, she shared how entire families are severely injured in motor vehicle accidents. Our police officers must deal with these situations on a regular basis. No one could imagine how damaging this could be until you experience it. I thought of the emotional stress it could bring to our officers, and due to that fact, I felt obligated to do something for them, as they do so much for our community and us. My service as a chaplain is a sense of gratitude to these men and women in blue.

I became a Volunteer Hospital Chaplain at Chesapeake Regional Hospital in Chesapeake, Virginia, in October 2018. While serving as a Hospital Chaplain, I met Mrs. Terry Haddock, who oversaw registering newborn babies in the mother-baby ward of the hospital.

In our initial conversation, she shared how she served as the senior Chaplain for the Norfolk

Police Department. She then shared how challenging the job of a police officer was. After our conversation, I became excited about becoming a police chaplain. Police chaplaincy seemed like a great opportunity, but more importantly, it reminded me of what Christ said, "He came to SERVE!"

Each time the senior chaplain and I would meet in the hospital hallways, she would share her different experiences with me as a Police Chaplain. I used to think the role and responsibilities of both hospital and police chaplains were one and the same. To resolve the confusion in my head, I asked a question to Chaplain Haddock, 'What is the difference between a hospital and a Police Chaplain?' She told me that there is a host of similarities, but her most important definition that grabbed my attention was, 'A Police Chaplain's primary job is a Ministry of Presence.'

It was about being there in a time of need. She began to give me data about police officers and their need for a Chaplain (Data like divorce, Suicide, Substance Abuse, and stress). What touched my heart most was when she shared how police officers must respond to cases when children are involved and the stress it places on our officers. After this conversation, I was convinced that I wanted to become a Police Chaplain.

### What do police chaplains do?

Chaplains build a link between police officers and the community. A chaplain is a person who comes from the community and works with them. So, they fill the gap between them. Police officers have always been considered tough and rough, and emotionless. But that is the requirement of their job. It does not mean they don't possess feelings. You can't take the human factor from them. They also get affected by their work. However, the chaplains working alongside the officers both develop relationships that allow the chaplains to get an insight into the officers' lives, and this would show the community police officers are kind-hearted people who have the mission of serving their community.

Chaplains play an important role in the lives of our officers. They give our officers the assurance that we will always be there for them in their time of need. Chaplains always make themselves available to our officers when they need someone to talk to. Since chaplains work with our officers closely, they become aware of all the strains and stresses of their life. Because of the closeness, the relationship can sometimes turn into a friendship between the chaplain, police officers, their families, and the civilian staff.

Police chaplains are involved in circumstances when a member of the staff dies in the line of duty. The chaplain's response must always be quick to serve and console the family. They empathize and give their willing support by visiting the family or the staff. The support of the chaplain is dedicated to the entire family.

Although the police chaplain's primary responsibilities are focused on the well-being of the staff, they also offer their support to the victim's family members if it is deemed necessary. If someone asks their opinion or advice about their religious faith, chaplains always look forward to helping.

Whenever there is an injury or sickness of a staff member during their service, chaplains will pay a visit to the staff member at home or in hospitals in order to express their care to them as well as to the families.

### *How Police Chaplains operate*

Police chaplains accompany officers on duty by going on a ride along with them. This allows the chaplain to become better familiar with the staff, and it can also develop a closer relationship between the two. Ride-alongs are the best way to understand the nature of their job and how every officer deal with the situations. The police chaplains are provided with personal protective equipment while riding with these officers on duty.

Chaplains come to the patrol divisions on a regular basis. Sometimes, they are assigned a designated shift with a particular police officer. In doing this, chaplains build relationships with the officers they serve.

Police chaplains are available, either on or off duty. They are also available for private meetings, depending on the staff's comfort level and a suitable environment. If there are departmental meetings, staff training sessions, events, or briefings, chaplains stand ready to attend them. This is all contingent on if it is appropriate and not highly confidential.

### *How to Become a Chaplain*

Most Chaplain positions are Volunteers. This includes most police and fire departments. Almost every hospital, Prison, Military, or Higher Learning institution requires chaplains to be ordained with a Master of Divinity Degree. These positions are mostly paid positions.

Almost every Police Chaplain is a volunteer, and most of them are Ordained Ministers. Practically every police chaplain will go through a criminal background check. They must also be in good standing with their church denomination. The police chaplain must also get approval from their local church body if they are a pastor of a church. As stated before, the primary mission of the police chaplain is to be a ministry of presence.

When I met Chaplain Terry, I was an Ordained Minister with the United Church of Christ. My professional experience started with the Marine Corps, where I served my country for twenty-two years and retired as a Sergeant Major. In addition to that, I also served as a pastor in Suffolk, and Chesapeake, Virginia.

Regarding my academic background, I have completed both an Associate's and bachelor's degree. My higher education included a master's degree in both School Guidance Counseling and Theology.

Let's discuss the steps taken into consideration when becoming a chaplain, which is as follows:

If you have the desire to pursue a career as a chaplain, there are certain steps you need to follow to meet the right qualifications. You must meet the job requirements to have a greater chance of employment in this profession.

### *Earn a bachelor's degree*

Most organizations and institutions prefer hiring chaplains with at least a bachelor's degree. Try to pursue a degree in counseling or theology. Focus on degrees that include courses like the history of the church, biblical studies, or worldviews. Courses in critical thinking are almost always preferred.

### *Go through Training*

Many local colleges, universities, and seminaries offer specialized chaplain training. Volunteering in a certain institution can be beneficial for you.

For example, suppose you want to become a professional hospital chaplain. You can make the best use of your undergraduate education by volunteering in a hospital. Most colleges and universities require students to do internships during their education phase to get a better understanding of the workplace. This kind of experience might increase your chance of getting a job at your preferred institution.

### *Pursue an Advanced Degree*

To create an edge, consider pursuing an advanced degree such as a master's degree in divinity, a Master of Science in spiritual care, or a Master's in a similar field.

Many institutions often require a master's degree or Ph.D. for chaplaincy positions, especially if you are considering serving in the military or hospitals. Even pastoral care and biblical counseling can also improve your resume for this profession.

You can also take the CPE (Clinical Pastoral Education) training which is required by most institutions. You need to determine first whether you need it or not. In this training, chaplains from different faiths join to share and learn about their real-world experiences and how they can apply them in their profession.

### Get ordained

In some scenarios, the employer might need you to get endorsed by a religious organization to become ordained. It would be best if you determine first whether you must go through this process or not. Even if it applies to you, make sure to know all the necessary steps so that you can meet the applicable criteria.

### *Certification*

You may need to earn the certification, which is recognized by the Association of Professional Chaplains. Some employers do prefer these certifications. What you need to do is to search for the right one based on your faith and career goals. Generally, a written test has been conducted to earn your certification.

All the degrees and certifications are the prerequisites for getting the job as a Chaplain. Sometimes, many institutions require you to complete the residency as well under the supervision of a Senior Chaplain.

The above steps will guide you on the things that need to be considered while choosing this path as your career.

Being a Police chaplain has been one of the most rewarding decisions I have ever made. For two years, I have been able to comfort family members after the loss of their fathers and mothers. I've been there for our police officers in their time of need and conducted funerals for families with no minister or pastor. Most of all, it has allowed the city of Norfolk, Virginia, to see the ministry of God working through me.

# Chapter 2
# My First Ride

I believe working in a new place for the first time brings excitement and a new learning experience for almost everyone. I feel privileged and proud to bring a lifetime of experience as a Police chaplain. I was extremely excited about it, which is why I arrived at the Second Patrol Division early on the morning of July 1st, 2021. As I got out of my vehicle, I adjusted my uniform, making sure my Gig line or military uniform alignment was perfect.

As I entered the double glassed doors of the patrol Division, my eyes darted from left to right at the Police Graduation plaques, and there were personal photo shots of each chief and assistant chief that had served the department devotedly through the years.

When I entered the building, my eyes were stuck on the wall that displayed photos and plaques of officers who had made the ultimate sacrifice for the whole community. This portion of the wall was dedicated to the Fallen Heroes of the Norfolk Police Department. I later found out that there were thirty-nine officers from the department had died in the line of duty. I felt a tremendous honor to be a part of such an honorable profession.

As soon as I entered the Roll call room, I found out that I was the first one to arrive. I scanned the room and took a seat at the back. Officers started arriving when the clock grew closer to 0600 (6:00 AM). Each one of them greeted me with good morning chaplain, as some simply stated morning chap., I greeted each officer with a smile and a healthy good morning, but it was a welcoming environment overall. And then it happened, the Corporal walked in, and you could imagine when a Marine General had walked into the room. Without saying a word, the entire room snapped to the position of attention. As they came to an attention position, so did I.

Then something very peculiar happened that took my attention. Each officer took out their small flashlight, turned it on, and shone it toward the Corporal as he watched. Later I found out this was a standard procedure to ensure each officer had a functioning Flashlight. The Corporal then gave the command to sit, and the officers and I took our seats.

The Corporal then began to give instructions concerning things to look out for during the shift. Next, he began to assign each officer their routes, including their patrol car numbers. He then welcomed the chaplain and told the team that the chaplain would be doing a ride with us today. He then looked at one of the officers, which seemed to have several years of experience. The Corporal informed the officer that I was assigned to him during the ride-along for the day. The officer nodded his head as if he was saying 10-4 (affirmative signal); I understand.

At the conclusion of the Roll Call, each officer made their way to a room called the equipment room. Once inside the equipment room, I could see the officers attaching a small wire cord to their uniform shoulders. I later found out that it was a video camera that could record their conversation when answering calls with the public.

One officer in roll call was assigned to manage the equipment room.

As my officer exited the equipment room, he smiled and said, "Are you ready, chaplain?" Filled with excitement and apprehension, I smiled back and said, "I am Ready!"

The officer I was assigned to, was tall with broad shoulders and had the demeanor of a strong man. He asked, "If I had ever ridden before?" and I answered, "No, Sir." Exiting the glass doors, we scanned the parking area for the police vehicle we were assigned. As we approached the assigned vehicle, I noticed the officer had done a complete walk around the police car. I assumed he was looking for visible dents and scratches on the sedan from the prior shift.

I noticed he paid careful attention to the tires as well. After inspecting the tires, he opened my side of the patrol car. I was amazed to see the computer system and all the communication equipment installed inside the vehicle. I continued to stand outside as he turned the different knobs and buttons that caused several quick blasts of several different types of sirens. This was fascinating for me!

Soon he turned a different set of knobs; I saw the various displays of blue/red lights on top of the vehicle. I looked again inside the vehicle and noticed a metal rack between the officer's seat and the passenger's seat. In the rack, there was a 12-gauge shotgun installed, and to the right of the shotgun was a military-style rifle called the AR-15. In the military, the same weapon was called the M-16A2 or the M-4. The difference between the two weapons was that the AR-15 could not fire fully automatically.

I watched the officer push one of the buttons on the control panel as he informed me this button would release the shotgun and the AR-15. Carefully he took the shotgun out and began to unload each of the shotgun shells to ensure he had all his shells. He did a safety check and placed the shells back in. He took the AR-15 out, did a safety check, and then placed the rifle back in the rack and locked it.

Once the vehicle inspection was completed, we got seated in the vehicle, and the officer started his sedan. After the sedan started, the officer began logging into his computer. Once he had successfully logged into his computer, I began to hear the radio dispatcher making assignments to different officers.

As we pulled off, we had only gone a short distance when we stopped in front of his personal vehicle; he showed me a device that would pop the back lift-up door of his sedan. The vehicle we were in was the Ford Explorer.

I watched as he took a huge military-style bag from his personal vehicle and placed it in the back of his sedan. In fact, as I looked around me, all the officers on that shift were doing the same thing.

I later learned that the bag contained a very intensive medical kit for emergencies. Once this was completed, we started on our journey. Before leaving the roll call, I was asked to end the meeting in prayer. When the officer and I departed the parking lot, this time, my prayer was silent. I asked God to cover us as we started our shift.

He picked up his radio microphone, and his first message to the dispatcher was, "Please note that I have the Chaplain riding with me on this shift." The dispatcher replied, "Signal-4", i.e., I copied or understood. There was silence as we pulled off, and I quickly thought about how I should break the ice and eradicate this awkwardness of silence. I decided to first explore the officer's world. So, I started our conversation by asking the officer, "How long had he served as a Norfolk Police?"

He was well into his second decade and seemed to enjoy his job. In fact, as he shared his story, he stated that he had spent the past several years as a school resource officer. Because of Covid-19, he was called back to the patrol division and placed back on the street as a patrol officer. I then asked him if he had a family in the area as I watched a huge smile come across his face. He stated he was married and had two lovely sons. He went on to share how he and his two sons loved sports. I could tell this was an officer who totally loved his family and dedicated his time to them.

During the ride, I heard different officers and dispatchers conversate. I never heard either the officers or dispatcher use the word 10-4 or any of the ten codes. The officer that I was riding with stated Norfolk Police does not use the 10-

code model; but uses Plain Talk communication, which I found interesting.

We received our first call, and it was a homeowner who arrived home from shopping and found her front door open. As we arrived, she was standing outside her home. Upon our arrival, a backup unit also arrived with us. Because the officer was not sure if the area was safe, I was told to remain in the vehicle until the area was deemed safe. Chaplains must always understand on a ride-along, the officer is in charge. From where I sat, I watched the officers enter the front of the home. Some officers went to the back of the resident. I must be honest; I was nervous as it seemed like hours that the officers were in and around the home. They were inspecting the entire house.

Soon the officers returned to the homeowner; the officers told me that I could step out of the patrol vehicle. Chaplains should always follow the instructions of the officer. As we all entered the residence, the homeowner was instructed to look around her home to see if anything was missing. One officer followed her throughout her home. I watched them go from room to room. In the end, she was given final instructions from the officers, which included safety tips for securing her home.

Once in the patrol vehicle, my officer informed the dispatcher that the home was secure, and I watched him make a written report on his computer. We departed from there, and my officer showed me how to check on the computer to see the pending calls from the dispatcher. He began to show me how to use the computer.

I felt like I had, for a moment, gained this officer's respect. I believe when chaplains follow the instructions given by the officers, it helps to strengthen the working relationship between the chaplain and the officer.

Our next call was from a senior citizen who called in and felt that someone had broken into her home and was hiding in her attic. As we arrived and after talking to the homeowner, it seemed as if she was suffering from dementia or Alzheimer's. A good friend of the homeowner was present to provide support to the homeowner. The senior was convinced that someone was in her attic. As the officers carefully made their way up the attic stairs, I took the time to comfort the homeowner.

Police Chaplains should work with their department to undergo Critical Incident Training (CIT). With CIT, seminary, and mental health training, I was able to help comfort this beautiful senior citizen. When the officers returned, they assured the homeowner that she was safe. I gave her my Chaplains business card as she felt much safer as we left her home.

Again, as we got back into the sedan, the officer shared with the dispatcher the senior's home was safe and secure. As we were on the road, we received a call for a vehicle that was parked on the side of the road, and the car had been there for several days with no attention. The officer began to tell me how many cars were stolen each day and then drove to different places and left.

He began to share how so many people leave their cars running as they dart into the home to just grab something, and as soon as they return to the car, they find their vehicle gone. When we arrived near the reported vehicle, we saw this car, and as the officer ran the Vehicle Identification Number, the information came back that the vehicle was stolen.

The officer gave me a quick lesson on what happens when a car is left abandoned or stolen. We stayed on the scene until a tow truck arrived, and the vehicle was taken away.

As my first ride-along ended, there was no doubt in my mind that I had developed a long-lasting relationship with the officer. We pulled back into the patrol division, and I was ecstatic about my first ride. Even my officer shared how he enjoyed our ride, and he looked forward to us riding again.

On my first ride, we did not discuss religion at all. But I know I have developed a lasting relationship with the officer. In fact, he and I would go on to ride together four additional times. I believe that in establishing a ministry of presence, chaplains and officers must first establish a working relationship together.

## My Second Ride

I want to share another ride-along experience where I saw the love of God in mankind. It was my second ride which occurred with a young African American young police officer. This officer was tall with a quiet demeanor. Born and raised in Virginia Beach, I could tell from our usual conversations that he was a solid student in high school.

Our ride together was a twelve-hour shift that started at 6:00 PM and ended at 6:00 AM the following morning. Part of our patrol beat covered a beach area called Ocean View. The beach parking lot was posted as off-limits to all vehicles at sundown. Individuals could walk on the beach all night, but parked cars were prohibited from sunset to sunrise.

We were patrolling the beach area at night when we spotted a vehicle parked illegally with the engine running. As soon as we approached the vehicle, the officer parked our car, where he could get a clear view of the vehicle and the license plate. The very first thing he did was that he picked up his radio microphone to call the dispatcher in order to get the correct information about the vehicle.

Once he had the information from the dispatcher, he began to exit his sedan. When he was getting out, I asked him, "Should I stay in the vehicle?" He answered me, "You can get out but stay well behind me." I did exactly what he had stated. As we approached the vehicle, we noticed five young men sleeping in the car. I further observed that all of them had close-cut haircuts, which gave me the impression that they might have been in the military.

The officer pulled out the flashlight and tapped on the window to wake the men up from their sleep. The man in the driving seat sleepily rolled down the window, and he seemed to be of Spanish descent. In fact, all of them seemed to be

Spanish. The officer asked for the driver's license and went on to say they were illegally parked. Then he asked all the men to step out of the car, and he checked each of their ID cards.

The officer called the names from their ID cards to the dispatcher to check their past records for any crimes. He then did a visual inspection of the vehicle. From the officer's observation, he could tell that the driver had been drinking.

Apologetically, the driver admitted that he had been drinking and his plan was to sleep in the parking area so he did not get a DUI (Driving under the Influence). It was our righteous observation when the driver explained the fact that all of them were associated with the Navy and had returned from an eight-month deployment in the Middle East.

During this whole scenario, in my mind, I wondered if the officer would charge the driver. After spending twenty-two years in the Marines, I knew a DUI charge on the young man's record would scare his military career for a long time. I remained quiet as the officer chatted with the driver. I pondered what the officer would do.

Almost at once, the young officer gained a tremendous amount of respect in my eyes after the decision he made. He asked the driver to call his ship and send them a van so they could go back to their ship without letting any other official figures know.

We waited there till the ship personnel came. The van took the men to the ship because one member of the ship drove the car back to the naval base. As we left the scene, I asked the officer, "Will you be a career police officer?" He stated Chaplain, "I am not sure." I knew this officer had saved the career of these young sailors. The whole situation would have changed if the officer had chosen not to empathize with those young men. These men would have lost their entire career as well as their reputation. A single act of kindness can go a long way.

*"A single act of kindness throws out roots in all directions, and the roots spring up and make new trees."*

*~Amelia Earhart*


I rode with this officer on several ride-along, and each time we rode, my goal was to see the characteristics of Christ in his service. Religion might not be discussed during a ride, but I feel it's a chaplain's goal to find the work of Christ in each officer.

## Things to Remember

- Chaplains must remember that the officer is always in charge.

- Always remember the Officers vehicle is the officer's office; remember to keep the passenger's side clean.

- Always follow the Officers instructions

- Get to know the officer's world first.

# Chapter 3
# Death Calls

Chaplains must be prepared and ready to answer different calls during a ride-along. Death calls can be incredibly challenging. Police officers are routinely exposed to these deaths and death calls. But they maintain their professional demeanor in any worst-case scenario to support the ones who need them the most. However, they must face these situations heroically and courageously. Chaplains ensure that they give their full support to the police officers and the families who have to deal with the traumatizing situation.

My first death call was a male, approximately thirty-eight years old. I was riding with a police officer when the dispatcher informed him that the medical staff had already pronounced the death of the victim. We were also apprised that two teenage children were the only family at home. On our way to the victim's house, the officer asked me, "Will you spend time with the children while I am conducting the investigation?"

When we arrived at the home, one police officer was already on the scene and told us which apartment the victim was in. As we approached the top of the stairs, I saw two teens sitting on the top of the steps. I introduced myself as the chaplain, and I sensed great relief on their faces. They asked if I would stay with them while they waited for the arrival of their family member as well as the funeral home. They informed me that their mom was out of town, and they were waiting for their aunt to arrive.

One of the children stated that their dad was wearing a gold chain, and the children wanted to ensure they received it. I informed them that once the funeral staff arrived, I would make sure I got it for them. While they waited, I asked the son and daughter, "May I pray for you?" They responded instantly, "Yes, Sir, please." We all joined hands, and I shared a prayer for their family.

When the prayer was over, I saw a small minivan arrive at the apartment complex, and I knew from their attire that they were the staff members of the funeral home. They were wearing black suits with white shirts. The two men stepped out of the van and walked up the stairs where the kids and I were sitting. Both introduced themselves as members of the funeral home staff. As the two morticians entered the room, I followed them.

The victim was on the floor, and I asked the funeral home staff if the children could get the gold necklace that was around the victim's neck. I looked at the table and saw several small lunch-type Ziplock sandwich bags lying on the table. As the mortician removed the gold chain, I reached for a pair of gloves which was on the back of my belt in a leather pouch. Chaplains should always make sure they always have latex gloves in their possession.

Once I had my gloves on, I took the gold chain, placed it in the Ziplock bag, and handed it to the son and daughter sitting outside on the steps. I then began to instruct the children on what was happening in the room with the mortician.

I shared that the funeral home attendants would have to bring their father out in a body bag and then carry him down the steps to place him on the stretcher.

I asked the children to move to a position at the side of the building so they would not see them bring their father out. However, they wanted to stay and watch the morticians take their father to the stretcher. Because of the size of their father, I asked the other two officers to give extra hands to bring the victim down the steps.

As soon as their father was on the stretcher, I went back inside the apartment with the children to ensure they were doing fine. I stayed with the children until the family member arrived at the home. Both son and daughter gave me a big hug and expressed their gratitude for staying with them. All the officers were also grateful for the chaplain being on the call. That's what chaplains are for. They must be ready to always help.

Death calls can sometimes be very strenuous. I was on a ride-along when we got a call that a family member had passed, and the son and daughter were waiting for our arrival. As we arrived at the home, I went to the children and said how sorry I was for their loss. I asked, "If there was anything I could do for them?" The daughter said with a quavering voice, "Will you just give me a hug, please?" She was crying, and I could see the pain in their eyes.

Not only did I hug her, but I gathered the son and daughter and asked if I could pray for them. The chaplain should always ask a family member if it is okay to pray. You can't just assume the family wants you to pray. So, you have to be cautious about it. I always make it my business to ask permission from the family first and then pray if they permit me. After the prayer, the officer and I entered the home.

As soon as we entered the home, I sensed an odor that I had never experienced before. For the first time in my life, I experienced the smell of death. The person had passed several days before the children found him. The body had already started decomposing.

The officer and I waited for the arrival of the Funeral Home Staff. As the funeral home members arrived, they went into the home to make their first assessment. After this, they returned to their vehicle and began to put on their protective white clothing. When the funeral home staff were transferring the remains, the officer assisted the staff and made sure that the remains were overseen with dignity and respect.

I remember having an experience with a homicide police officer. This happened in August of 2021. I received a phone call from one of our homicide detectives to ask if I would accompany her to give a death notification. A young man had been killed on the street, and his parents were about to be notified of his death.

In our conversation, the detective shared that the young man killed was very close to his parents and an only son. His mother was recovering from a serious illness, and the deceased son had been instrumental in his mother's recovery. In fact, the young man was a motivational factor in his mother's wellness.

The father had already been informed of his son's death, but because of his wife's illness, he felt he needed help sharing this information with her. He also requested that the detective bring a chaplain to share the death notification with his wife.

I knew this notification was going to be very emotional. Getting dressed, I asked God to speak to my heart, giving me something to say that would help this ailing mother.

I got dressed in my full-service A uniform. I grabbed my minister's manual and darted to the Police Operations Center. When I arrived at the

POC, I walked the long hall and headed to the homicide division, where I met the detective and her staff. We left and headed to her vehicle. The ride to the victim's home was short, and the father was waiting for us at the front door. When I stepped out of the vehicle, I could see the blank stare on the father's face.

The detective introduced me to the father, and we entered the home. One detective went with the father to their son's room while the father instructed us to keep straight down the hall, and the bedroom door to his wife's room would be open.

We entered the wife's room, and before the detective could introduce herself, the mother's eyes became fixed on the shiny crosses on my shoulders. The mother bawled, "Why is the chaplain here?" She then asked anxiously, "Is my son okay?

The detective introduced herself and then introduced me as one of our chaplains for the police department.

The mother's concern was heightened, and she asked again, "Is my son okay? The detective wanted to console her and took the mother's hand in hers. I took the mother's other hand in mine. The detective opened her conversation with "I am so sorry!" as she began to share about her son's death.

When the word death was mentioned, the mother screamed, and I held her hand a bit firmer than before. For a moment, both the detective and I remained silent as the mother's emotions were overwhelming. As chaplains, we must always give a family member time to grieve.

At one moment, she reached out to me with open arms, and without wasting a second, I hugged her. I promised her that our Chaplains Corps would be there for her throughout the whole process. She was sobbing and said, "Thank you very much." Then I shared with her that I would like to bring our senior chaplain to meet her on the following day. She agreed and seemed to be satisfied that we were coming back to her home on the following day.

I asked the mother if I could share the 23rd Psalm with her, and she agreed. As we were about to leave, the detective asked the mother if she wanted the chaplain to share a prayer with her.

She nodded her head yes. I took her hands in mine and went to the Lord in Prayer.

I called our senior chaplain to give her a brief of the notification when I reached my home. We made plans to visit the family the next day. The senior chaplain decided to get lunch for the family from Olive Gardens. As we both arrived in Full-Service A uniform the next day, the family expressed their feelings to the senior chaplain about how grateful they were for my visit and prayer. The senior chaplain shared with the family that I would be the point of contact for the family. The senior chaplain had prayer with the family as we were about to leave home. My heart went out to this family, and it seemed I was the only one they trusted. I could feel a strong connection growing with this family.

For five days straight, I visited the family. I was truly touched when the mother and father asked me if I would go shopping with them to find a suit ensemble for their son's funeral.

I arrived the next day at their home in a blue double-breasted suit. While at the men's store, I was taken aback when the mother said to the salesperson, "I want a suit for my son that resembles the suit the chaplain is wearing right now." I felt humbled and honored by this request.

I had recommended the store to the family because even I had gotten my suit from the same store. They were concerned about their son's size for his suit. I stepped away and called the funeral home. The funeral director informed me of the size we should get.

The family then asked me again if I would accompany them to make funeral arrangements for their son. The next day we sat in the funeral director's office as he asked the family if they had a minister to conduct their son's funeral. The family clearly stated, no!

The funeral director looked over at me and asked, "Chaplain will you be willing to conduct the funeral service?" I answered earnestly, "I will be honored if the family would like me." The mother started to cry and said, "We would love the chaplain to conduct the funeral."

I believe I was able to help lift the burden of the death of this family's son. The mother said something that was carved into my mind and soul. It will stick with me for the rest of my life. I remember she said, *"Chaplain Hall, you have been our Guardian Angel!"*

As chaplains, our primary duty is to support the men and women and the families of our police department. There are times when the community will need our services. As chaplains, we must be ready to answer the call. Jesus said,

'I did not come to be served but to serve and give his Life as a ransom!"

~Mathew 20:28

**Things to Remember**

- Chaplains can play a vital role in a death call.

- The chaplain should always carry latex gloves.

- The chaplain should carry a list of the different Funeral Homes in the local areas.

- The chaplain must always ask a family member if they would like prayer. Never pray without asking.

- Be patient and give time to the person to grieve.

# Chapter 4
# A Ministry of Presence

Our lives have become too much isolated and individualized. We are more engaged with machines rather than the people around us. The world is revolutionizing, yet the irony of the situation is that we are involved with new technologies and machines and are getting away from people. We become secluded, and people are less likely to take any help from others. Therefore, they must deal on their own with the problems and difficulties of life. It is pivotal to have God's presence all around.

The times when something terrible happens without giving any warning or intimation. Whether it would be the loss of a dear one's life, a drastic accident, or someone who has to deal with a chronic illness, you find yourself unaccompanied. You have no idea what you are going to do or how you are going to cope with this situation. The pain, agony, and mental trauma would break your entire courage, and it would feel like this pain wouldn't go away, and you couldn't handle this.

When such circumstances arise, words are not as enough as the presence of another person to console those who are dealing with this ordeal. If you know that you are not alone in this situation, and there is a mental satisfaction that someone is there to care for you, this feeling is transforming. Most often, you wouldn't know whether you would be able to make it through the night, but the feeling of transformation would give you hope that you would survive this situation. This would represent the call to ministry.

It means it is a call to get engaged or involved in the lives of others. It is more like a commitment to be there for others and give them a feeling of personal presence. When you are more concerned about being present in someone's life and choosing the right words, ministry turns out to be more powerful and meaningful. Actually, God is the one who models and values this kind of ministry.

And if you talk about the presence of God, you can feel his presence by being near to his people and promoting love and care to his people. Even if you understand this simple understanding of the nearness of God, then you will also contemplate the true meaning of chaplaincy.

Chaplaincy provides a compassionate and empathetic presence to those people who are vulnerable and in need of spiritual care. The ministry of presence is a prospective result for chaplains who are true to everyone, including their selves. As chaplains, you don't have to act or be in the persona of a 'caring person.' It is about being true to yourself, and in this way, you can be embraced by others.

The role of police chaplains starts to evolve from bringing the blessings of God to strengthening the police officers as well as communities to cope with the struggles and difficulties of life. Chaplains are not bound to a particular church, but they hold the concept of the ministry of presence. Their presence serves the purpose of providing comfort and care to people who are in a vulnerable state. It doesn't matter whether that person is living a spiritual life or not. Their job is to be there and show love to those who are dealing with difficult circumstances, even to those who don't believe in God.

It has been said that most Police Officers are unchurched. If I talk about my experience, I rode with these young men and women fifty-four times, and I can confirm that the name Jesus Christ was not mentioned most of the time. However, as I rode with these hometown heroes, I made sure to make it my mission to see if I could see the love of Jesus Christ working through these men and women. The word religion was rarely talked about, but even Jesus was not big on Religion.

Nonetheless, occasionally, you experience something that leaves a mark on your mind and soul, and you cannot be able to forget it. I want to share the same ride-along moment which I saw in a young police officer that has been truly stuck in my mind over the past year. In fact, I can't even remember his name, but I truly remember the actions he took. I was astonished to see the love of Jesus Christ through his people.

This ride-along took place with a young white male officer who treated me with such respect. I was truly excited and felt at ease riding with him as we took off from the patrol division.

It was one sweltering hot August evening when this officer signed in and alerted the dispatcher that he had the Chaplain riding with him. I remember as soon as the dispatcher called back to him on the radio and stated to respond to a certain area of the city and be on the lookout for an elderly African American female who was suffering from Dementia. This senior lived alone, and the next-door neighbor would check on her daily. The neighbor followed her and tried to convince her to please turn around and return home. The officer said, "Chaplain, we will head in that direction."

As we were on our way to the destination, I wondered how this young man would handle this kind of situation. I knew the young man had gone through Critical Incident Training (CIT), but there was so much going through my mind. As soon as we got closer to the street, I could see a staggering image coming down the street. When we were about to reach there, the image became clearer, and I could see this was an elderly female.

The heat that night was blistering. As the officer turned on his lights and the sedan came to a stop. The lady seeing the blue lights caused her to stop also. My heart skipped a beat as this lady reminded me so much of my grandmother, who had raised me for the first eighteen years of my life. Now, I was more interested to know what would happen.

I wondered how this young man would deal with this old lady who may have been three times his age. But what I acknowledged from this young man truly amazed me. He empathized with her and showed the utmost respect, which was commendable. He spoke to her as if she was his very own grandmother. He talked to her with so much love and care. I could see the characteristics of Christ truly running through this young man.

In about five minutes, he had convinced her to let him put her in his patrol vehicle and take her home. As an act of chivalry, I remember he opened the sedan door for her. This senior was so frail that this young man picked her up in his arms and put her into the back of his vehicle. Then carefully, he strapped her in with the seat belt.

I witnessed the pure love from God, and I thought to myself, "God is still speaking." To encounter this kind of experience, your words are not enough to express your emotions. For a second, I became speechless, as if there was a large lump in my throat. Then a neighbor came up with his car, and we followed him to her home.

When we arrived at her home, I stepped out of the sedan and immediately opened her side of the car door. The officer unbuckled her seatbelt as the neighbor opened the senior's front door. I watched this young man pick the senior up in his arms and literally take her into her home, and then he would sit her in a chair.

I was amazed and yet astounded to see this. What I saw next made me know There Is a God! He went to the refrigerator and found a bottle of water, brought it back, opened it, and gave it to her so she could drink it.

I immediately thought about what Jesus said. "Giving someone a cool glass of water would not go unnoticed." I had never seen anything like this. As she was drinking, he got down on one knee and shared with her his concern for her medical condition. He then asked her politely if he could call the paramedics to take her to the hospital. She agreed, and the medical staff was there in less than five minutes. As I watched them move her with such tender care, placing her on a stretcher, I knew God's Love was being shown that evening. Most often, you experience such events in your life where you feel a connection between the gratifying moments of life and the presence of God. This was one of those moments where I truly felt that "God is with us and within us."

"I will never leave you nor forsake you."

~Hebrews 13:5, Joshua 1:5

You can feel the presence of God in different ways. Sometimes, you feel the presence by seeing someone comforting the needy one or in a home where happiness and love are showing. Chaplains work through this ideology to help others and to promote selfless love and care. In this way, you can see the love of God.

Some of our Police officers may be unchurched, but in the Norfolk police department, I continue to see the love of God working through these young men and women every day. For the actions of these men and women, I am convinced that the Norfolk Police Department stands Second to None!

# Chapter 5
# Riding With Female Officers

My first ride-along with a female officer occurred on July 9th, 2021. As usual, I arrived for roll call and reported to the Street Sergeant's Room to check in. During the Roll call, the Sergeant welcomed me. I shared with the Sergeant that I wanted to ride that evening with the Blue Sector, which started at 1800 (6:00 PM). The Sergeant gave me the name of the officer with whom I had to ride and then stated this was a female officer.

The Female Officer was short in stature, but her uniform was impeccable. Her stance and the immaculately clean and tidy uniform were the first noticeable thing. As we left the equipment room, she asked me, "Are you ready, Chaplain?" As we headed to the parking area, she told me with a slight warming smile, "Chaplain, we are going to have a good night. I was amazed by the fact how young she looked and willingly she came into this profession. As we started our ride, I asked her how long she had been with the department. She told me that she had only been a police officer for two years.

The conversation between us began, and I was becoming intuitive to know her more. I then asked, "Do you like being an officer?" She passed an approving smile, and I could sense that she loved her job. I asked her then, "Did you enjoy the Police Academy?" She stated that she started her academy but had some challenges. She further added that she had completed about half of the instructions; she took leave and returned at the start of the next academy.

By hearing that, I gained a tremendous amount of respect for her. It takes a lot of courage to come back after fighting your struggles and fears. It let me know this officer was no quitter.

Our first call from the dispatcher instructed us to respond to a home where a teen may have assaulted his girlfriend at his home. As we arrived, we saw that the two teens were in the yard along with the male teen's mother. I observed how this officer handled the situation was very mature for her age.

I watched her conversate with the mother and teen, and she oversaw the situation quite easily and within a short span of time as if she was a well-experienced officer. The girlfriend of the teen had walked several miles to see the male.

To make sure the female got home safely, the officer put her in her sedan and took her home to her family. I was genuinely impressed with the officer as she reached the young teen girl's home. The officer expressed empathy toward the young girl and advised her on a personal level. She even gave her a business card if she needed to talk to the officer. This showed that the officer indeed was concerned about this young lady, and it showed her love for mankind.

The officer stated that we were going to a home to present a warrant to an individual to report to the court. When we arrived there and started to walk towards the door, she then gave me my first instructions. She shared with me that we should never stand directly in front of a door and that it would always be safe to stand to the side. She also advised me never to stand in front of a window. This officer was a quick thinker and had excellent command over the rule of law. There is no doubt that this young officer will have a fruitful future, and I look forward to seeing her in a leadership position soon. She was very decisive in her decision-making. I rode with this officer ten times more, and my admiration for her leveled up every time.

## Second Female Officer Ride

My second female ride took place on September 6th, 2021. This was a ride with the 1st Patrol Division Red Sector, which started at 1900 (7:00 PM). This officer was a mature female who had gained much respect from many female officers. New and young female officers would look up to her skills and courage. Again, this officer's uniform was very sharp, and I could tell she knew her job and had strong leadership skills.

When we initiated our ride, I asked her if she had a family in the area. I got a huge smile as she began to tell me about her family. This relaxed me a bit when the officer let their guard down and opened up to me. She talked about her husband, and I could tell she was deeply in love and had found the man of her life.

I then asked if she had children, and she said yes, one. She then asked if I wanted to see her baby. I said yes, as she leaned over to show me a picture. I was making an image of a kid in my mind, and when I saw the picture, it was a huge Great Dane! She said proudly, "This is our baby!" I was amused and beamed with joy.

This officer was a quick thinker with sound judgment. I rode with this officer on a number of ride-along. However, there was one call I would like to share where I could encounter several times the love of God in this officer.

We received a call to report to a home where a son and daughter had gone to visit their elderly father. On their arrival, they found their father to be non-responsive. When we got the call, the medical staff had pronounced the death of their father. The daughter was standing outside the home waiting for us as we arrived.

The officer approached her and asked the daughter if there was anything we could do for her. The daughter said with a despairing sigh, "Will you hug me? The officer opened her arms widely for her and hugged her tightly, and I followed next. We then went into the home.

There was an odor when we walked into the house that I had never experienced before. It was my first experience with the smell of death. The officer informed me quietly that it'd been several days since his death.

We then waited outside for the arrival of the funeral home staff. As soon as they arrived, we also entered the home with the funeral staff. I saw that the funeral staff went to their vehicle outside and donned their white protective suits. The officer, who wore only gloves and a mask, went in with the funeral staff to ensure the deceased was handled with the most dignified respect.

When we headed out of the house, I told the officer that what she had done inside had gone beyond her call of duty. What she told me touched my heart deeply. She said, "Chaplain, I would want someone to treat a member of my family the same way.

I rode with this officer again, and she shared with me a call that she, along with her partner, responded to the night before our ride. They responded to a call where a victim was stabbed near a local park. When the two officers arrived at the spot, they found a young man with multiple stabbed wounds. I was able to watch the video cam as this young man's entire body was soaked with blood.

In the footage, the two police officers diligently handled and treated the young man in a way that seemed like the two of them were actual doctors in a trauma room. The wounds of this young man were so severe I could see it was hard finding the punctures. Literally, the officer's hands were covered with blood.

It was a life-and-death situation, and I could see the efforts they were putting into saving this young man's life. These two officers were doing everything so they could rescue this young man.

The officers were waiting anxiously for the paramedics to come, and as soon as they arrived, I watched them put the young man into the ambulance. I then had a view of the trauma room as well, where the doctors and nurses were giving chest compressions to restore his heartbeat.

My female officer watched with anticipation as the medical staff tried their best to revive him. After what seemed like an hour of chest compressions, the young man was pronounced as dead. For almost two hours, this female officer had to sit in the trauma room with the remains of this young man because the investigation process had begun.

During our ride, when we talked about this situation, I saw tears filling up in the officer's eyes as she looked at me and said chaplain, "No one deserves to die like that." My heart went out to her at that moment. In the media, we constantly see the negative about our men and women in blue.

This book is written to let the community know that what I just shared is happening across the country by police officers everywhere. Officers save the lives of the communities they are sworn to protect. But today, it's about the Norfolk Police Department, Norfolk, Virginia.

This officer displayed the characteristics that Christ would want in each of us. Once again, I saw Norfolk Police Department at its best.

In November of the year 2021, I rode with another female officer. She was young and had been an officer for two years. Like the other females, her uniform was perfect. She had a quiet demeanor and was female of discernment with an eye for quality. She was a solid leader, like a good Marine.

As a Marine Sergeant Major, I felt I had a good judgment on solid leadership. She was a great teacher. She knew that I had attended Radio class, and during the ride, the dispatcher assigned one of the officers in our area to report to a scene. The officer handed me the radio microphone and said, "Chaplain, I want you to give our number and say signal 2." I remember I asked her, "Are you sure you want me to do it?" She looked at me and said sternly, "Do it!". She said it as if she was a Sergeant Major. I picked up the microphone, gave our number, and said signal 2. Signal 2 was letting the dispatcher know that we were the backup unit for the officer responding to the call. She smiled and said, "Good job, chaplain!" To hear such appreciative words from that female officer, I was on cloud nine.

I stated several times that Religion might not have been mentioned or discussed, but every time I rode with these hometown heroes, I saw the love of God in every one of these officers.

In May of 2022, I was given a chance to ride with a female supervisor. I had spent all my time riding with junior officers. Now I had the opportunity to see how a supervisor operated during a shift. This was quite a massive experience for me. I rode with a corporal who was an Air Force Veteran. I watched her during roll call, and I could tell she cared about her officers. She had a calm way of carrying herself, but she led with such confidence and dignity, which was quite commendable.

After the Roll call, she shared that she had some paperwork to complete and that soon she would join me. The moment came when we started our ride-along. At the very start, her focus was totally on the computer system. She took her time as she began to give me detailed instructions on the system.

I could tell she wanted me to become fully acquainted with the program. Her instructions made me feel like a student in school. She then asked me to share what I had learned during my different ride-along.

She made it her business to make sure my ride-along was positive. During the whole night, she kept me focused on the computer. During our ride, we would report to different scenes that officers were responding to. She was able to provide each officer with positive leadership and professional advice. This was a true leader in every way.

I said this initially; I wrote this book after riding with some of the most professional men and women under God's Heaven. It has been a true pleasure working alongside some of the best police officers on this side of heaven.

## Things to Remember

- Never stand directly in front of doors or windows.

- Always stand to the side.

- One thing was particular about female officers, i.e., their focus was always on teaching.

# Chapter 6
# Ride Along during An Arrest

Police chaplaincy has an amazing opportunity to serve the officers who are committed to serving the community and society. Riding along with the police officers every day presents the ministry of presence because every day, chaplains encounter lost trust that can be built, closed hearts that can be opened up, and injured souls that can be healed. Chaplaincy brings the opportunity to promote hope, and grace on every call, at every turn, with new officers every day.

Working closely with the police officers, I comprehend the struggles, frustrations, and dangers associated with this job. I greatly respect and appreciate their selfless work and devotion to the community. A chaplain's basic priority is to help and support them while they are engaged in protecting and serving this community.

Our nation's courageous police officers face a lot of challenges as daily they have to deal with deaths, destruction, devastated victims, and every worst possible criminal activity that you cannot imagine. This stressful and demanding work negatively affects them emotionally, spiritually, physically, and mentally, as also their relationships. Chaplains help them in decreasing stress and pressure so they can do their best at their jobs.

Police chaplains serve all kinds of support in different key areas of law enforcement as well as the communities they serve. These areas are not limited to only the well-being of the officers or spiritual support. In times of need, they show their extra support to bring out the best in the situation. Sometimes, police chaplains go over the board to foster a strong relationship with the police officers.

Chaplains become a resource to police officers and personnel as they work directly with them in order to deal with the demands and stress of law enforcement. The work of a chaplain depends on the relationship they build with law enforcement officers. This can only happen when the chaplains engage in building a foundation of trust while encompassing the needs of the people under stress and assisting the police officers in any kind of crisis situation.

During my 500 Hours of riding with Norfolk Police, there were several occasions the officer I was riding with apprehended a suspect. During these times, chaplains are uninvolved. I made it my business to keep quiet and safe and maintain a professional distance as the officer made the arrest.

Most chaplains in most states are not allowed to be armed with any type of weapon. This is true for the city of Norfolk, Virginia. When chaplains ride with a prisoner in custody, the chaplain must remember never to get personally involved with the person being transported. On a few occasions, I have been asked by prisoners for prayer. My job is to get the officer's approval always before praying. With the officer's approval, I would pray for the prisoner from my passenger seat.

On each ride-along, I know my safety rest in the hands of the officer I am riding with. My personal oath to God is always to do my best to stand ready to support every officer I ride alongside. Chaplains know that with every ride-along, the danger would accompany them around every corner. Like police officers, chaplains conduct ride-along because of their dedication and devotion to the city and the police officers they are sworn to serve.

When chaplains accompany officers to the city jail, it gives the chaplain the privilege to meet certain staff members of the Sheriff's or Corrections office. In addition to meeting officers of the prison, chaplains also get to see how the magistrate system operates. This overall allows the chaplain to gain knowledge of how the city functions.

I accompanied the officers I was riding with to their court appointments on a few occasions. Police Officers are called to the courts every day for warrants or arrests, which they had done it weeks before. Again, when chaplains accompany officers to court, the chaplain gains a host of knowledge concerning the Judicial system.

I remember riding with a female officer when we received a call from the dispatcher to report to a hotel in the area and to be on the lookout for a suspect, perhaps armed with a weapon. The (BOLO) "Be on The LookOut" gave us a clear description of what the suspect was wearing. As we arrived at the hotel with a backup unit, we spotted a young man that matched the description of the BOLO report. When the young man observed us, he took off running in a full bolt! Then two officers took off running towards the suspect.

Seeing the officers in action, I started running along with them. The two officers cornered the suspect. The backup officer had the suspect's right hand and tried to put it behind the suspect's back to be cuffed. The officer I was riding with was helping the backup officer, providing full support to each other. The suspect was trying to reach inside his waistband forcefully with his left hand. This young man was at least 6'1, and about 250 pounds. The whole time, my eyes were focused on the suspect's hand as he tried to reach his waistband.

My natural response was to reach and grab the suspect's wrist to hold it for a few more seconds so that my officer could secure it with handcuffs. It was a natural response for me as I was concerned for the safety of my officers. I remember the backup officer showed his appreciation and said, 'Thank you, chaplain,' as they led the suspect to the patrol car. A search of the suspect's body revealed no weapon, but the situation could have turned in a different direction if anything had gone wrong there.

I know this was not in the chaplain's line of duty, but I knew these officers would gladly lay down their lives for my safety. I felt it was my obligation to protect the safety of the officers I swore to serve. Once back at the patrol division, the word was quickly passed throughout the division to the officers. If you get in a situation and need assistance, the chaplain is willing to step in and help. I gained a lot of respect from the officers in the division. I believe the chaplain's goal is to support our officers and the city we serve.

Immediately following the incident, I called and notified my senior chaplain of my actions. The senior chaplain and the officers on the scene informed the street sergeant. It was the first and only time I assisted an officer in response. But I believe it was for a worthy cause.

In 500 hours of my ride-along experience, I have seen the worst scenarios that police officers have to see regularly, how humans become inhuman: murder, suicide, deaths, heart attacks, an overdose of drugs, and whatnot. I have to disclose the news to the family member that your child, partner, or friend won't be coming home. I have to give immense support to the police officer who has seen so many crimes repeatedly.

Without a doubt, this has been by far the most intense ministry and also the most gratifying and rewarding. I chose to assist those who serve and protect this community without thinking about their own lives and continue to do so. I prefer to help and assist those who are grieving, who have lost their faith, and who are mentally disturbed, whether they are police officers or civilians.

**Ride With Shots Fired**

As I mentioned earlier, during any Ride-Along, danger could await the Chaplain around every corner. During my ride, I often heard over the radio, "Shots Fired!". This happened when I was riding with a female officer, the dispatcher assigned us to a call where an individual had been shot. During a call of a person being shot, it causes the officer to respond to the scene "Code-3". When responding to Code-3, the officer implements blue lights, a siren, and a speed, most of the time above the posted speed limit.

The officer was short in stature, but the way she handled the police vehicle at a high rate of speed was astounding. I remember she even asked me, "Chaplain, are you okay? My answer to her was with confidence as I stated, "I am fine." I showed my calm exterior, but I must say my heart was racing. I had never been in a vehicle at a high rate of speed. However, I totally felt safe with her. This ride gave me a rush of euphoria after seeing people moving their vehicles out of our way so that we could travel swiftly to our destination.

I had heard how NPD (Norfolk Police Department) provided outstanding training to the officers in Defensive Driving. The officer's driving skills proved she excelled in this training. As we traveled to our destination, the dispatcher constantly updated us on the situation. As we got closer to our scene, the dispatcher put out a BOLO Report on what the suspect was wearing. Officers are always supposed to be on alert. As we were about a block away from home, my officer spotted an individual who fit the description of the suspect.

She stopped the sedan swiftly and instructed me to stay in the vehicle as she left the sedan. In no time, the backup joined her as they approached the suspect. I saw them as they talked to the individual. Soon another vehicle arrived, and the individual was placed in the sedan. The individual was taken to be questioned.

As my officer came back, we went to the victim's address.

The area of the victim's house was taped off with 'crime scene tape.' I saw a female crying near the scene, and I asked my officer if this could be a relative of the victim. We found out this was the wife of the victim. I asked the lead detective if I could approach the wife for prayer. He approved my request as I made my way to the wife. When I approached her, I introduced myself as the chaplain and asked her if I could pray for her. She approved my request; I took her hand in mine and said a prayer to Lord.

There are days when there is so much sunshine in the duties of the Police Chaplain, but there are days when storm clouds arise. On those days, it's so good to know we have a God with us who will stand by us even until the very end. This ideology will give you the strength to overcome difficult situations.

Police Chaplains have the ability to bring healing through their presence, simply working for the ministry of presence and promoting love and care to the law enforcement officers and the community as well. Chaplains don't solve the sufferings of the survivors, neither they eliminate the revulsions. However, they could listen to the agonized voices. They could validate their emotions. They could offer their prayers. They could give their undivided attention. They could offer their presence in difficult and challenging times so that they don't feel alone, lost, and lonely.

First and foremost, Chaplains understand we are not sworn officers of the law. We also know our obligation is to serve the men and women we are sworn to help. Chaplains working alongside our law enforcement officers build relationships. Building strong relationships will help bind the two entities together. In this way, it creates strong trust. For the chaplain, trust from the officers allows the chaplain to present a true **ministry of presence.**

Often people wish to be at the scene of incidents or crimes and see exactly how things are being handled by the Police Department. Ride-along with police officers gives a whole new insight into the department. The way police officers are dedicated to their jobs is commendable. Their devotion toward the community and nation is contagious. This book would help everyone to see the other side of the coin.

## Things to Remember

- Chaplains in Norfolk, Virginia, are not allowed to be armed with any type of weapon.

- Riding with the prisoners in custody, the chaplain must remember never to get personally involved with the person being transported.

# Chapter 7

# Police and Community, Building Bridges Together

In the early days, the police department or law enforcement officers were present only to protect the community, prevent crime or enforce the law. But now, as the world is revolutionizing, things are changing for the betterment of society and police officers. Now, the police department feels the need to change the ideology of enforcing the law not only by protecting the community but also by maintaining a trustable relationship with the community.

In general, police officers have that image in the mind of the community members that they are rigid and hard to approach. The people don't trust the law enforcement officers and feel threatened by them. It is because the police officer's job involves a lot of critical incidents and accidents like murders, brutal deaths, robbery, and a lot of other hate crimes. Their job makes their skin hard, but it doesn't mean that they don't feel anything. They possess a beautiful heart, just like any of us in the community. They are a part of the community and should be treated like an 'extended family member.'

For example, when you are home, you feel safe because you are surrounded by your family members who protect you no matter what. However, if you are out of the house or go to the office, college, school, or anywhere, then it is the police officer's job to give you protection and give you the feeling that you are secured by them. This is why they are an extended family member of the whole community.

One of the crucial factors that play a vital role in successful law enforcement is strong police and community relations. It is imperative to build good community-police relations to develop trust between the community and the police.

If a citizen work along with the police officers, the police work becomes more effective. If people may not feel safe, then police officers are actually fighting an uphill battle to solve the crime without any support.

We found that there is always a gap between the community and the police officers. The police department is currently working to strengthen this bond because now there is a massive need to fulfill it. Chaplains are the solution to this particular problem as they are the binding blocks that connect the police officer with the community.

Chaplains foster the relationships between the police officers and the people of the community. Their relationships sometimes become impaired because citizens have limited access to and knowledge about the police department's functions. And as part of their job, police officers often are restricted due to their job requirements.

In this case, the chaplains come into the picture and build a strong relationship between the community and the police officers. They fulfill the spiritual and emotional needs of the two entities, which include police officers and community members. The police chaplains become a connecting link that fills the gap between them.

Therefore, the community receives the emotional support that they want at conflicting times, and the police officers can do their job effectively by not compromising their emotional needs. The chaplains form a communication link between the police officers and those affected by the crime.

The citizens often see chaplains as more approachable. Due to this advantage, they hope that their involvement with the police officers makes the law enforcement officers more approachable as well.

The role of a chaplain is to connect the police officer and the community members together. They provide their full support to the police officers and citizens in the time of their need. Chaplains perform the task of a social, spiritual, and emotional nature. On the other hand, police officers perform a task that requires law enforcement. As a result, the chaplain's role is more like a 'balancer' between law enforcement officers and the community.

Chaplains work for the ministry of God; they work devotedly to serve civilians and police officers by giving them appropriate assistance, comfort, advice, and counsel to those in need who might need extra support.

Several programs have been established in the city of Norfolk to create a partnership with the various faith-based community members to respond and support the police officers in providing a better quality of services to the public and community.

The goal of these programs is to eliminate the gap between police officers and citizens and to respond more comprehensively during times of crisis or incidents.

The city of Norfolk is surrounded by several cities that make up what we call the "757". These cities include Chesapeake, Portsmouth, Virginia Beach, Hampton, Newport News, and Suffolk.

Of all the cities that are mentioned above, very few are faced with the different challenges that the city of Norfolk faces. Norfolk is considered mostly Urban with a Suburban feeling.

Norfolk is 46.32% White

40.59% Black

5.90% Two or more races

3.67% Asian

One of the reasons I decided to become a Volunteer Police Chaplain with the city of Norfolk was because of its programs designed to bridge the relationship between the police department and the city. As a new chaplain for the department, I was curious about the different programs that the police department had implemented to bring the two groups together.

The division of the police department that manages the police-community relations program is called "Prime Affairs." This is the Police and Community Relations division of the department. It is led by a strong police captain who served several years as a United States Marine. He leads with a firm hand. In addition to the captain, a police Sergeant is second in command and would have been an outstanding Marine leader. The very first community relations program that caught my attention on my arrival was called "*COPS AND CURLS.*"

This was a program designed by the police department as a formal night out for young girls whose fathers were incarcerated. The essence of this program is to fulfill the emotional needs of young girls who do not feel alone or lonely as their fathers were not with them.

The department takes some help from the vendors with providing evening gowns for these beautiful young girls for a night-out gala event. One would say this was a 'prom-type program.' Most of these young girls were very young. The program includes games, dancing, and dinner. Police officers volunteered to make sure the girls had an evening that was filled with fun. For these young girls, this would be an evening they would never forget. As a father of five daughters, I thought this was pure ministry.

This is what God would want us to do. On my arrival at the department, Covid-19 soon followed. Because of this horrific Virus, the program had to be postponed.

Another program that I fell in love with was the Norfolk Police Ice Cream Truck program. This was a standard Ice-Cream truck designed to support community events that would provide free Ice Cream during a community event. The truck drew the attention of both children and adults from every community in the city. This is a program that the community truly loves and engages the community members well together.

Another program that the department uses is called the "PALS" program (Police Athletic League). This program happens each summer when the police department brings children of elementary, middle, and high school to the training division for two weeks. Elementary students have two weeks, then middle, then high school students meet. The kids arrive from 8:00 AM to 5:00 PM each day. The program focuses on leadership skills, character development, and wellness for the body. The program is designed for both boys and girls. As the chaplain, it's a true honor to be part of this program with community affairs.

Another program the police department uses to support the community is called "Community Walks." If someone is injured or a death occurs by gunfire in a community, police officers will walk that community, knocking on doors to provide the community with safety literature provided by the Crime Line department. Information on providing safety tips and crime line phone numbers is instructed to families. Children and adults are given coupons for a free soft drink at their local 7-11. More importantly, the appearance of police officers walking in the community gives the community the assurance that the police are there for them.

The Norfolk Police Department is making every effort to develop a solid working relationship between the police and the community it serves.

Several weeks ago, I had the incredible opportunity to attend a Hispanic culture event at a Spanish church in Norfolk. I was attending the event with the community service Captain. The event was truly outstanding, as we both were given a chance to speak to about three hundred people. This was the best way to communicate with the people and know their difficulties and fears. Most often, lack of communication creates a lot of problems, and to solve this problem, events like these can help in filling the missing link.

The last community program I would like to introduce is the Norfolk Police Department Civilian Police Academy. This is a program the Police Department sponsors to bring community members to a small, modified police academy. This is a three-month program where the community gets to witness first-hand selected police department training. A Spanish version is also provided to Spanish-speaking members of the community.

At every church and major community event in the city, the Norfolk police department makes it their business to have a representative from the police department.

The reason to incorporate these programs is to maintain a strong relationship by building mutual trust between the police officers and the communities they serve. This will also promote transparency which is crucial for positive community-police relationships. Suppose any critical incident happens, the people will trust the police officers, and they will not feel that the information provided to them is purposefully hidden or withheld from them.

As a chaplain, I work with all the community members and police officers despite having different religions, faiths, races, or skin colors. The police officers also receive training on diversity and cultural competency to communicate well with people of various ethnic backgrounds or cultures to reduce the communication gap.

Even these programs are designed in this manner to make a connection between the community and police officers. Due to these programs, police officers become more visible in their communities, and they might get a chance to know their residents. People don't get an opportunity to interact with police officers outside of the law enforcement context.

As a result, people make negative assumptions about police officers because they only interact with each other if an individual has a parking ticket or has broken the law in any way. The programs help the communities, police officers, and chaplains to interact with each other in a non-enforcement context. This will break down the stereotypes associated with police officers, and the community will not feel hesitant in approaching them. It will allow law enforcement officers to know more about law-abiding citizens and which neighborhoods are high crime areas.

Norfolk Police Department has a strong Public Information Division. This division is managed and run by a solid media group. At every community event, you will find this group taking pictures and making videos to post on the Norfolk Police Department website and Facebook page. The world can see NPD working tirelessly to bridge a strong working relationship between Norfolk Police Department and the city it's sworn to serve.

I have worked with these police officers, and I can say that these police officers work day and night to preserve the peace and bring positive change by taking care of every member of the community.

# Chapter 8
# Officer's Well Being

There is no doubt that the job of the police officer is stressful and challenging, with the highest physical and mental health hazards, if we compare it with any other profession. This issue cannot be taken lightly or unaddressed, as it has many consequences. As a result, the job performances of police officers decline, and their ability to make decisions is impaired. Eventually, everyone associated with them gets negatively affected by their mental and emotional state.

It is a predominant need to invest in protecting and maintaining police officers' mental and emotional well-being. Now, it has been recognized that the role of a police officer's wellness plays a vital part in police work, so several programs have been created to promote and preserve the emotional and physical health of police officers.

The Chaplaincy program is one of the programs that has been established to provide additional support to the police department and their families. Chaplains from different backgrounds, faiths, and values satisfy the needs of a diversified workforce and the community as well because they are linked together.

The role of a chaplain is to provide spiritual and emotional support in times of crisis or stressful situations. They become a trusted source through which officers and their families can easily talk about their issues and concerns. As chaplains also hold the privilege of legal confidentiality, this fosters the space for law enforcement officers to seek guidance and assistance with professional and personal issues.

Why is Spiritual support needed? As many officers have different religious beliefs, the chaplains provide non-religious kinds of support. The aim is to provide the care and love they need during challenging times. The chaplain's work is to promote the Ministry of presence and a belief to help, guide, heal, nurture and reconcile everyone.

Every police chaplain's worst nightmare is to be awakened in the middle of the night with a concerning call of an injury or death of an officer. The chaplain's daily prayer is that each officer returns home safe and sound at the end of their watch.

During my 500 hours of ride-along, unfortunately, I received two calls in the middle of the night regarding the well-being of our officers.

My first call came when one of our detectives was approaching a suspicious individual. The Individual fired several rounds at the detective. From the phone call, I was informed that the officer was hit and immediately taken to a Norfolk hospital. I sighed with relief, "Thank God!" At least they have taken him to one of the best Trauma hospitals in the region.

There was no further information provided on the call about the health of our officer. My mind was racing while getting dressed in my class A uniform. "How serious was the officer's condition?" Questions, assumptions, and doubts were generated in my thoughts. I was worried about his condition.

After getting dressed, I hurriedly made my way to the hospital. The route to the hospital became the longest route for me; I wanted to be there as soon as possible. On my arrival at the hospital, I saw that the hospital was surrounded by police cars all around. As I exited my vehicle, I went straight to the hospital's emergency room.

There were at least twenty-five to thirty police officers outside the ER room with concerned looks. I made it my business to quickly go to each officer to shake their hand. They all greeted me with a hello or evening chaplain. My goal was to observe the expressions on each officer's face. While I was observing their expressions, there was a blank stare on each of their faces. None of them knew the condition of our officer.

One detective stated, "Chaplain, the chief was in the ER waiting room area." As soon as I moved in the direction of ER lobby, I saw the chief, along with the deputy chief, standing in the lobby area. As the chief spotted me, he walked toward me and stated, "Officer was hit, but his condition is not life-threatening." Only my heart knows what a relief it was to listen to this news. I felt a burden had been removed from my chest. I said, "Thank you, Jesus!!"

By then, our senior chaplain had arrived on the scene. The chief then said to the senior chaplain, "I am sure the officer would love to see the chaplains." We made our way to the trauma room where the officer was placed. As we walked into the room, I noticed that room was full of police officers that were friends of the wounded officer. The senior positioned herself near the officer's head, and I made my way beside the officer's soon-to-be bride. The officer shared the whole incident with the senior chaplain. He told her how three rounds were fired at him; the protective vest stopped two of the rounds, but one bullet made its way under the neck area of the vest, which made its way into the shoulder area of the officer.

The officer was extremely pleased to see us. After a short conversation with the senior chaplain, she asked me to lead the room for prayer.

I said, "let us pray." Everyone in the room lowered their heads while I prayed. We then left the crowded room, and I left with gratitude. I thanked God for watching over the young officer. Every officer in the police department realizes that no matter what time it is, their chaplains will always be there for them.

The shooting took a toll on the wounded officers and several of the officers that were involved in the shooting. Emotionally and mentally, the officers were drained because of the shooting.

I am so grateful that Norfolk Police Department has an outstanding "Peer Mediation Program." A few weeks later, I was notified by the Officer in charge of the Peer Mediation Program that we would be having a Peer Mediation Round Table session with the officers involved in the shooting. I remember the day of the session, and

I was asked to open the training with prayer. There were seven officers, along with the officer in charge and a mental health counselor, who also joined the session. For almost three hours, each other got to express their emotional pain. By the time the training session ended, each of us was left with a feeling of solace, including the Chaplain.

My second call came in the middle of the night because one of our detectives was involved in a motor vehicle accident. Because several gunshot victims were admitted that night, every ER in Norfolk was full. In that situation, a rapid response was required, so our detective was transported to another city, seventeen miles away from Norfolk.

When I got the call, I dressed and went to the hospital. I was taken to the trauma room when I arrived at the hospital. Our Chief of Police was standing at the officer's side. The officer's wife was also in the room. Both the officer and chief thanked me for coming. After some conversation, I asked the officer if I could pray for him. As he agreed, I took him by the hand and went to the Lord in prayer.

There is no doubt in my mind that my presence as a chaplain for the Norfolk Police department has been instrumental in the well-being of our officers. I said earlier in the book that the chaplain's goal is to bring a ministry of presence. Sometimes it's not about rendering a prayer or giving words of condolences. Sometimes just the presence of the chaplain, just being there, is enough to bring God's presence into the situation.

## Crisis Intervention

Mental illness is a significant concern across the United States. Police officers experience a high level of stress, anxiety, and trauma daily, which has an adverse effect over time. This cumulative effect of stress might happen when the officers are involved in critical incidents on a frequent basis.

The WHO (World Health Organization) also talks about mental health and considers it an important factor in the productivity of an employee. As far as police officers are concerned, they tolerate the pressure caused by exposure to high-stress incidents repeatedly. This can result in depression, anxiety, and PTSD.

To cope with this problem, several training programs have been established by mental health experts who comprehend the severity of this profession and their situation. The Chaplaincy program is one of the programs by which chaplains can apply their knowledge in adversity, stress management, and emotional distress.

Almost in every ride, I heard either the dispatcher or an officer mention someone struggling with mental illness. I was amazed at how often I saw or heard officers taking someone to the community service board to be evaluated for a decision to be taken to the hospital. Some cases were so bad that the Officers had to take the person straight to the hospital.

Crisis Intervention Training (CIT) is a huge part of the Norfolk Police Department. The course is a 5-day training now conducted at each Police Academy Class. I remember attending the class with one of the academy classes.

According to "Crisis International," CIT is a community partnership of law enforcement, mental health, and addiction professionals, individuals who live with mental illness or addiction disorders, their families, and other partners to improve community responses to mental health crises.

I felt CIT training was some of the best training I have ever encountered. During the 54 times I rode with these officers, I saw CIT being used almost on every ride. There were times when officers asked me to step in to add advice during several of the calls I was riding with.

The city of Norfolk is home to the largest Naval base in the world. The base population includes more than 82,000 active-duty personnel, 112,000 family members, and 39,000 civilians. This data is as of Jan 2021. Many of the active-duty members have faced war during the past several years. Because of the war, the military members and even their families have to face mental illness. I have been on several calls where a military member faced mental illness.

PTSD is a huge concern in the city of Norfolk. The local schools at all levels have their share of cases of students facing mental illness. Every school level has special counselors ready to counsel these students. Many students are placed on "Individual Education Plans." Each IEP is carefully put together and designed for each student. Sometimes the students become so emotional that officers are called to intervene and help protect both the student and the school. Even each hospital has a ward designed for mental health.

I believe that because of CIT training, so many situations have been handled by police officers calmly and efficiently. Police officers today are not only serving to protect the community they are sworn to serve but they are called upon to do so much more. It is beyond their responsibilities, showing a high level of humanity, love, and care. Police Officers also play a significant part in the mental health of the people they serve.

Police chaplains are also trained to work alongside each officer to be a partner in mental health. This is another way chaplains build bridges to join law enforcement, clergy, civic leaders, and the community, all working together as partners.  For the Chaplain, building these bridges is a sure way for the chaplain to introduce God as a ministry of presence.

Made in the USA
Middletown, DE
25 February 2023

25614355R00086